Elephant Line Up

By JONATHAN PEALE

Illustrated by TOM HEARD

Music Produced by ERIK KOSKINEN and
Recorded at REAL PHONIC STUDIOS

CANTATA
LEARNING

WWW.CANTATALEARNING.COM

CANTATA
LEARNING

Published by Cantata Learning
1710 Roe Crest Drive
North Mankato, MN 56003
www.cantatalearning.com

A note to educators and librarians from the publisher: Cantata Learning has provided the following data to assist in book processing and suggested use of Cantata Learning product.

Publisher's Cataloging-in-Publication Data
Prepared by Librarian Consultant: Ann-Marie Begnaud
Library of Congress Control Number: 2015958224
 Elephants Line Up
 Series: School Time Songs
 Retold by Jonathan Peale
 Illustrated by Tom Heard
 Summary: A song that teaches students how to form a line.
 ISBN: 978-1-63290-612-0 (library binding/CD)
 ISBN: 978-1-63290-570-3 (paperback/CD)
Suggested Dewey and Subject Headings:
 Dewey: E 395.5
 LCSH Subject Headings: Courtesy – Juvenile literature. | Students – Juvenile literature. | Courtesy – Songs and music – Texts. | Students – Songs and music – Texts. | Courtesy – Juvenile sound recordings. | Students – Juvenile sound recordings.
 Sears Subject Headings: Helping behavior. | Courtesy. | Students. | School songbooks. | Children's songs. | Folk music.
 BISAC Subject Headings: JUVENILE NONFICTION / School & Education. | JUVENILE NONFICTION / Music / Songbooks. | JUVENILE NONFICTION / Social Topics / Manners & Etiquette.

Book design and art direction, Tim Palin Creative
Editorial direction, Flat Sole Studio
Music direction, Elizabeth Draper
Music produced by Erik Koskinen and recorded at Real Phonic Studios

Printed in the United States of America in North Mankato, Minnesota.
072016   0335CGF16

ACCESS THE MUSIC!

SCAN CODE WITH MOBILE APP

CANTATALEARNING.COM

Have you ever seen how elephants walk? They like to march in line as they **stomp** along. Sometimes, at school, you need to walk in line, too, just like elephants.

Now turn the page, and get ready to line up and march. Remember to sing along!

Here come the elephants.

We're lining up at the door.

Here's one elephant.

6

Here's another one.
Here come more and more!

Here come the elephants.
Our **trunks** are **mighty** fine.

8

They swing out wide,
moving side to side.
They help us stay in line.

Stomp, stomp, stomp, stomp.

Stomp, stomp, stomp, stomp.

It's time to get in line!

Here come the elephants.

We're walking down the hall.

We weigh a **ton**, and everyone is walking quietly, straight and tall.

Here come the elephants.

We march along the ground.

Our mighty feet
keep up the beat,
but no one hears a sound!

Stomp, stomp, stomp, stomp.

Line up quietly.

Stomp, stomp, stomp.

Can you be quieter?

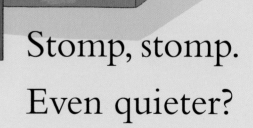

Stomp, stomp.

Even quieter?

Stomp.

17

Stomp, stomp, stomp, stomp.

It's elephant time!

Stomp, stomp, stomp, stomp.

It's time to get in line!

Here come the elephants.
Come join our **caravan**!

We march for fun,
and when we are done,
we're back where we began!

Stomp, stomp, stomp, stomp, stomp.

Stomp, stomp, stomp, stomp, stomp.

Stomp, stomp, stomp, stomp, stomp.

Stomp, stomp, stomp, stomp, stomp.

SONG LYRICS
Elephants Line Up

Here come the elephants.
We're lining up at the door.
Here's one elephant.
Here's another one.
Here come more and more!

Here come the elephants.
Our trunks are mighty fine.
They swing out wide,
moving side to side.
They help us stay in line.

Stomp, stomp, stomp, stomp.

Stomp, stomp, stomp, stomp.
It's time to get in line!

Here come the elephants.
We're walking down the hall.
We weigh a ton, and everyone
is walking quietly, straight and tall.

Here come the elephants.
We march along the ground.
Our mighty feet
keep up the beat,
but no one hears a sound!

Stomp, stomp, stomp, stomp.
Line up quietly.

Stomp, stomp, stomp.
Can you be quieter?

Stomp, stomp.
Even quieter?

Stomp.

Stomp, stomp, stomp, stomp.
It's elephant time!

Stomp, stomp, stomp, stomp.
It's time to get in line!

Here come the elephants.
Come join our caravan!
We march for fun,
and when we are done,
we're back where we began!

Stomp, stomp, stomp, stomp, stomp.
Stomp, stomp, stomp, stomp, stomp.
Stomp, stomp, stomp, stomp, stomp.
Stomp, stomp, stomp, stomp, stomp.

Elephants Line Up

Americana
Erik Koskinen

Verse 2
Here come the elephants.
Our trunks are mighty fine.
They swing out wide,
moving side to side.
They help us stay in line.

Verse 3
Here come the elephants.
We're walking down the hall.
We weigh a ton, and everyone
is walking quietly, straight and tall.

Verse 4
Here come the elephants.
We march along the ground.
Our mighty feet
keep up the beat,
but no one hears a sound!

Verse 5
Here come the elephants.
Come join our caravan!
We march for fun,
and when we are done,

GLOSSARY

caravan—a group of people or animals traveling together on a long trip

mighty—very great and strong

stomp—to walk with heavy steps

ton—2,000 pounds

trunks—the long noses of elephants

GUIDED READING ACTIVITIES

1. School is not the only place people line up. Can you think of other places where people get in a line?

2. Elephants walk in a line. What are ways other animals might move?

3. Lines can be straight or curvy. Draw straight and curvy lines on a piece of paper to make a design. The lines can be different colors.

TO LEARN MORE

Ponto, Joanna. *Being Respectful*. New York: Enslow, 2015.

Rustad, Martha E. H. *Elephants Are Awesome!* Mankato, MN: Capstone Press, 2015.

Smith, Sian. *Manners at School*. Mankato, MN: Heinemann-Raintree, 2013.